Decorative Needlework

May Morris

Decorative Needlework

By May Morris.

1893.

English Embroidery (about 1340) Portion of a Cope, "Free of Jesse."
South Kensington Museum.

Dedicatory Note

These pages are written for and dedicated to those who, without much previous knowledge of the art of embroidery, have a love for it and a wish to devote a little time and patience to its practice. The booklet does not profess in any way to be exhaustive, but should be useful as a keynote to further study, having been written from practical knowledge of the subject.

I have tried to show that executive skill and the desire of and feeling for beauty, realized in a work of definite utility, are the vital and essential elements of this as of all other branches of art, and that no one of these elements can the embroideress neglect or overlook if her work is to have life and meaning. If she pursues her craft with due care, and one might even say with enthusiasm, however, she will not only taste that keen pleasure which every one feels in creative work, however unpretending, but the product will be such as others will be careful to preserve: this in itself being an incentive to good work. For work done at the demand of fashion or caprice and that done inevitably, that is, for its own sake, are as widely dissimilar as can be: the first being discarded in a month or so as ridiculous and out of date, and the other remaining with us in all its dignity of beauty and fitness, to be guarded as long as may be against the unavoidable wear and tear of time.

Decorative Needlework

Chapter I. Historical Glance

IT is only of recent years that the art of needlework has come to be divided by a hard and fast line into plain sewing and embroidery. The two branches of the art are to my mind, and indeed used to be in practice, so nearly akin that the one merges into the other, and it is surely equally desirable to teach both. For it has become inevitable now-a-days to set about teaching this art as well as many another more important; the training formerly obtained by patient practice and watching a good method of work in a studio or 'workshop' (as they did not mind calling it then) being beyond the reach of most young people in these days, when apprenticeship is confined to mechanical trades, and is almost entirely discarded by artists. In past times it was natural and instinctive to decorate one's stitchery; a seam or hem would have some little touches of the needle beyond the mere piecing together or turning in of raw edges: from this stage grew the enrichment of hanging or robe for avowedly decorative purposes, but it should be noted that all the decoration had meaning in its beauty. I will not stop here to consider this phrase, which will be referred to later on in discussing the suitability of embroidery to various objects. Well, now-a-days, almost the only article of stitchery in which the two branches of the art, namely, plain sewing and embroidery, are wedded, is in the body-linen of a very fine lady, who loves to accumulate dainty linen round her, fine as gossamer, wrought by what under-paid work-girl she does not know or care. The following lines from a popular fashion-paper describe with unction the beauties of such garments: ' The night-gowns are remarkable for their exquisite work, the dotting all hand-wrought, the tiny a jour veining appearing between the pleats . . . and so forth ad nauseam.

But the hurry of modern life and the advent of cheap machine-work have, between them, done away with any leisurely decorating of garments except for the very rich ; and, as aforesaid, plain-sewing is taught apart from decorative embroidery. The instinctive desire of man to ornament whatever article he makes with his own hand, to place his mark upon his handiwork, leads him to decorate his clothes and other possessions as soon as his primitive wants are assured, and he leaves the first stage of almost unreasoning savagedom. The early Eastern civilisations availed themselves abundantly of this art, and their chronicles record many instances of the skill of Babylonian and Egyptian workers, and of the beauty and costliness of embroidered stuffs made in those countries. Egyptian textiles and needlework were eagerly sought after by other peoples, especially by the Jews and Tyrians. The great merchant-city of Tyre, capital of Phoenicia, ' the renowned city strong in the sea,' was indeed a centre of all the arts, whither treasures and produce of all sorts poured in from every imaginable land. She is threatened with destruction in the height of her prosperity by the prophet Ezekiel, who describes graphically her trade development, and the perfection to which it is brought. With that versatility of a travelled people which made them their renown, the Tyrians assimilated the arts borrowed from Egypt and Babylon, and, among others, the art of embroidery, which was much in demand, being most rich and beautiful, we are told. I must refer, too, to that already often-quoted passage in Exodus about the building of the temple; where the Jewish tribes doubtless placed, as an offering to their Jehovah, all the precious things they had brought away from that wonderful land, wise in all the arts of life, where they had lived so long. Among these treasures there are beautiful embroideries and cloths of gold, either brought with them or fashioned by themselves through their acquired knowledge ; rich hangings for the tabernacle, a veil for the ark, and robes for the high priest, all wrought with the splendour of colour and wealth of work which Eastern nations still cling to.

Greece and Rome, too, made abundant use of needlework, and hundreds of quotations bearing on the subject could be made from their authors were it within the scope of these pages. But between the poetry of the ancient, and, frankly speaking, conjectural art, and the tangible reality of the mediaeval, classical times lose their interest to a certain extent, and one is glad to turn to a period of that art which repays all thought and search and fills one with joy, to the art of the middle ages, namely, the XII. to XIV. centuries, where everything is instinct with life and originality in the handiwork of man. From these times (say from the XIV. century until now), the progression is also downwards, with reference to this art at least; and though for a long, long while later professional skill is so well-rooted as to become greenly traditional, design and invention are less markedly beautiful, and the early simplicity slowly gives place to a luxuriance and lavishness that marks the beginning of all decay.

For any one anxious to follow up this line of study in detail, it can be done to a certain extent by merely walking through our South Kensington Museum, to go no further, carefully noting and comparing the fine examples of early work displayed there. The great Syon cope is in itself a master-piece of design and workmanship, and is worked in a peculiar manner, to which I may have occasion to refer in speaking of methods of work. This cope is an often-quoted example, whose history in brief is that it was given by Henry V. to a convent at Isleworth at about the year 1414, though a piece of XIII. century work. The nuns of Syon led a wandering life, and, in Elizabeth's reign, travelling far and wide, finally reached Portugal, where they settled themselves. It is not long since that this their great treasure came back from Lisbon to England, to be wondered at in a dusky corner behind a glass case in a great museum.

It will be noticed that most of the fine early embroideries preserved to us are ecclesiastical, but it is not to be inferred from this that the houses and clothes of our forefathers were as bare of such decoration as our own. They naturally lavished their most costly and effective work on the buildings and vestments dedicated to their religion, but did not themselves, therefore, go without rich ornament. There are existing certain inventories and descriptions of the hangings of hall and bower, cushion coverings and so forth, that give us a delightful glimpse into the interior of a well-to-do house of the middle ages, and of later times also. Loom tapestry was of course often employed for such things, but being essentially laborious and therefore costly, worsted or linen hangings, rather roughly worked, often took its place, and in old inventories we often see such work minutely described. Very gay and pleasant an old hall must have looked on a festival day (and holidays were very many and more generally kept in those days), the rough stone walls hidden nearly roof-high by the warm coloured folds of stuff embroidered with fair roses, or ' portrayed full of woodland trees,' with perhaps a bordering of scrolls and shields with the possessor's device displayed upon them. Window seats and chairs would be fitted with embroidered cushions, screens and settles hung with gay cloths, and even the ' napery' or table-linen would not escape the busily plied needle.

As aforesaid, later work gradually degenerates ; even the splendour of embroidered apparel at the French and English courts under Henry II. and Francis I. and Henry VIII., respectively, verges perilously upon the vulgar in its extravagance. Coats and robes are loaded with work and jewels wherever it is possible to display either, until the unlucky bearers of these stiffly built-up garments look ridiculous far more than magnificent. Very handsome work is, of course, often to be met with at this time, but the tendency, on the whole, is towards display and grandeur, and leaves far distant the repose and gravity of the best times. Thence our glance travels onward until it comes to actual ugliness and vulgarity in the latter half of the XVIII. century - 'the great century,' as people were fond of calling it. But though the rich and important work is displeasing, we find a great deal of modest art that is delightful; flowery cloths and aprons worked by ladies at their leisure, or great bed-quilts and hangings, ingenuous and simple as regards design, but really prettily coloured, and stitched with some art.

So much for a brief glance at the growth of decorative needlework. It may seem at first sight unnecessary, but indeed could not be dispensed with. Even the slight guidance thus afforded as to the periods wherein to look for the best style, in order to study it, is a great help to the student while taste is being formed. Moreover, I find that in most people's minds there exists great confusion as to what is definitely the best work artistically. Few go back beyond the queer jumble of traditional design of the early XVIII. century, or the handsome florid renaissance styles of the XVI. and XVII. centuries, to the simple dignity and graciousness of mediaeval work. It is here, to the Middle Ages, I repeat, the student must go for example and inspiration towards serious work : modern embroidery does not compare favourably with that of any period, but it is the very antithesis to the early art, and it is indeed time that something was done to raise it to a higher level.

Chapter II. Embroidery Stitches. Chain-Stitch, &c

THE foregoing slight sketch of the history of embroidery will give some idea of what can be done and what has been done with the needle alone, or with the needle and a few tools of the simplest description. There are two sides to the art of embroidery. It may be considered as a pictorial art in which the material used serves merely as a surface or ground to be entirely covered with work, like the canvas of a picture. It may also be considered as a decorative art by means of which a woven stuff is ornamented with borders and designs more or less elaborate, but the textile used not playing so entirely subordinate a part as in the former case. The more important and pictorial side is usually left in the hands of professional workers of experience and skill, but the decorative and more popular work is quite within the scope of amateurs, and is indeed often more beautiful as mere ornament, though its intellectual value may not be so great.

Embroidery can be worked loose in the hand, or stretched in a simple frame, the stitches for the two methods sometimes varying. Fine and elaborate work, especially where gold thread is used and much moulding or relief required, should always be put in a frame, a smooth and evenly tight surface being very necessary to this class of work, as well as greater freedom of hand. Some stitches, on the other hand, are only suitable for work done loose in the hand, such as chain-stitch (when done with a simple needle) and several other looped stitches, also darning, stitching, and so forth.

Before setting to work, the learner has a few technicalities to master, and in the course of her work will encounter many difficulties, to be gradually overcome by practice and carefully corrected errors. For instance, there are certain definite stitches or sets of stitches to be learnt. These are learnt far more easily by word of mouth than by book, of course, and it will not be found advisable to burthen the memory at the outset with a long list of apparently fantastic names of stitches. To take them easily and

Decorative Needlework

quietly, I will devote a few pages to chain and other ' looped ' stitches, and the various purposes to which they have been and may be put.

Chain-stitch has been so called because it imitates, more or less, the links of a simple chain. It is the foremost and most familiar of all similar stitches. It has a very definite character of its own, and though apt to become a little monotonous, is from its laborious and enduring- nature well suited to work that may be subjected to much wear and tear. In the accompanying diagram it will be seen that each little loop grows out of the last; the needle follows the exact direction in which the line of stitches is to lie. Some of the most famous work in the world has been wrought in this stitch, and many important pieces remain to show us what can be done in the way of minute and laborious work combined with good design and beautiful colour.

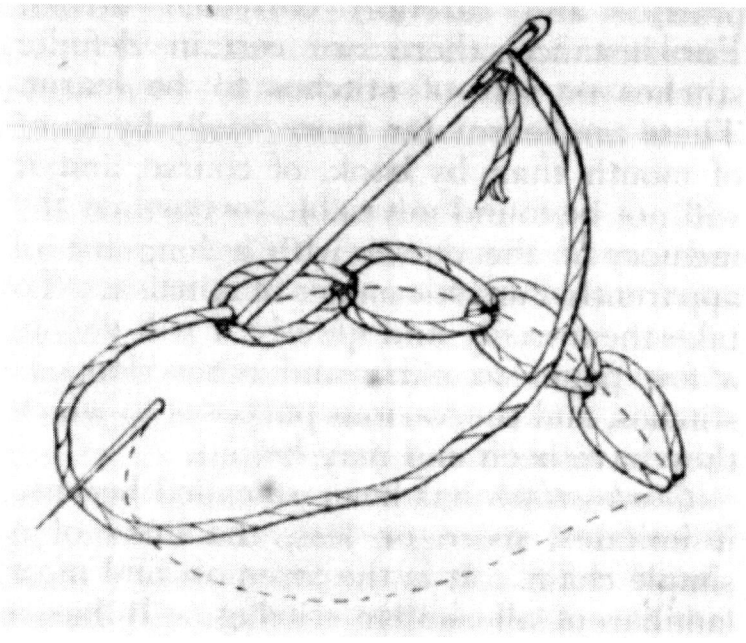

Fig. 1. - Chain Stitch.

The best way of using chain-stitch when the design is required to be filled with solid work is to start round the outline and work from without inwards, the result when finished being a series of curved lines, as indicated by the dotted lines in the diagram.

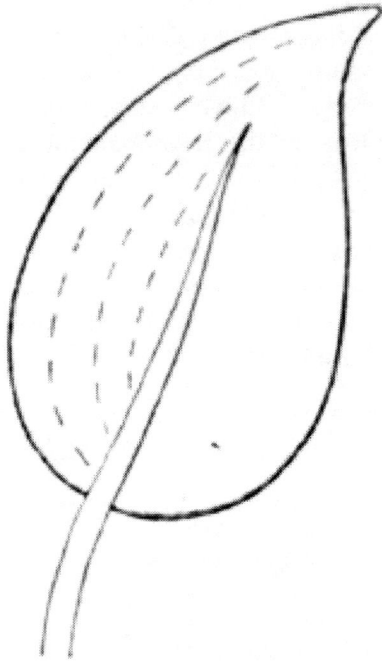

Fig. 2.

A good look at a piece of Eastern chain-stitch embroidery will teach more than any descriptive writing; and, supposing that you have such a piece before you, in the showcase of a museum, or, better still, in your own hands for closer inspection, you will note with what certainty and regularity the little flowers are worked, and how suitable this stitch is for long stems and lines. A great deal of the Eastern work on fine muslin that we see in such abundance in all shops now, is worked in some kind of tambour-frame ; that is, worked on a rather open stuff stretched tight, the thread being passed through and back with a hook or tambour-needle. It is not difficult to tell this work from the slower needle chain-stitch, as the former has a certain unmis-takeable evenness and flatness, which the other has not. The great cope of Syon that I have referred to already, is principally worked in chain-stitch, but worked with the most inconceivable minuteness, and here and there displaying a daring and originality never ventured on now-a-days. The little figures of saints and angels, for instance, have the faces worked in a peculiar manner, starting from the high light on the cheek-bone, and thence round and round outwards from this point to nose, chin, and throat, the features being outlined with a fine dark thread. This method of using chain-stitch for figure-work requires to be seen to be understood, and I would not recommend a student to attempt to apply it to her own work, as it is not adaptable to any modern style, and needs both the verve and simplicity of mediaeval design to carry it off.

I have in my mind, too, as an example of chain-stitch, certain work done in India in the XVI. and XVII. centuries for European buyers. It is very different in style and character, and has not, as it were, the intellectual qualities of the ecclesiastical work spoken of above. It usually consists of large hangings and quilts for beds of state, worked on a fine cotton ground entirely in chain-stitch of one colour. Very rich and effective does this work look in a brilliant yellow with an irregularly stitched background pattern also in yellow. These hangings and bed-coverings were ordered for state gifts or marriage gifts, the centres being sometimes occupied by the arms and device of the prince or lord for whom they were intended, elaborately interwoven with the design.

Of other stitches looped on the surface we have button-hole stitch, sometimes prettily used for the outlining of flowers and leaves. This stitch does not allow of much variety, and being rather hard and unpli-able, looks best in combination with other stitches. The same may be said of different lace stitches, which look well in moderation, and add variety to the work, but, having a rather mechanical surface, are a little wearisome if too much used.

Decorative Needlework

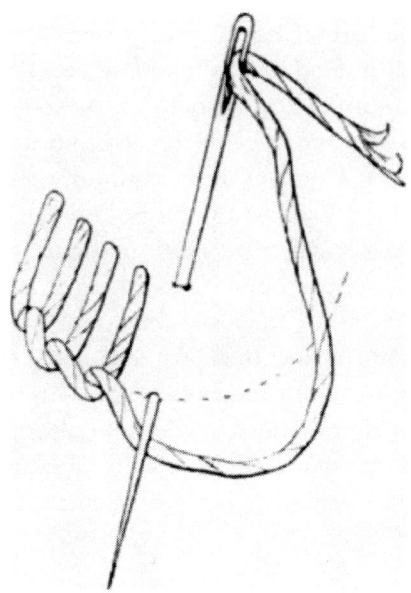

Fig. 3. - Button-hole Stitch.

Feather-stitch, familiar to the seamstress, is sometimes used for edgings and borders, and sometimes as a light filling of stems.

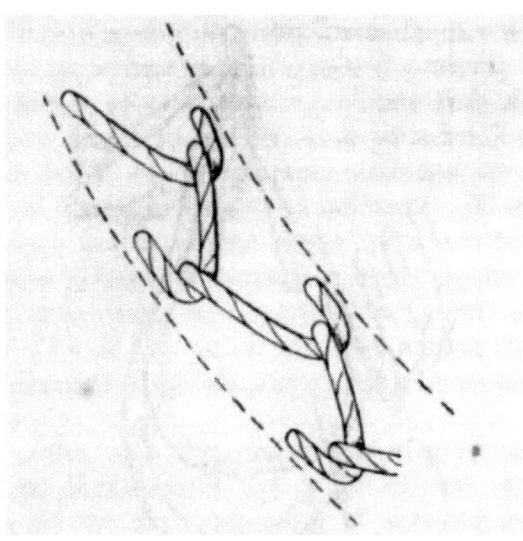

Fig. 4.- Feather Stitch.

Decorative Needlework

It bears no resemblance to the 'feather stitch' of the old writers, which is another thing altogether. The diagram will, I should think, sufficiently explain its nature.

Knotting or French Knot consists of several loops taken round the needle and secured by a stitch. This is effective for thick raised work, for the filling of flower centres and so forth, but is also seen in flat embroidery, such as some of the old Chinese work, which is sometimes composed entirely of very fine knots in different shades of silk. It is also seen used with comical effect in certain late English work, for hair, for trees, or sheep's fleece, or anything, in short, in which the embroideress thought a highly broken or granulated surface would help out her descriptive effects. Such 'effects,' however, are, to my thinking, in bad taste and out of place in embroidery ; where, even in the pictorial side of the art, natural objects should be interpreted by bold and skilful drawing, and no attempt at faithful copying be made.

Fig. 5. - Knotting.

Satin-stitch can be done in the hand or in a frame. It consists of stitches evenly laid in one direction, the needle passing under and over the space to be covered, back and front being similar. In the diagram the stitches are shown laid far apart for the sake of clearness, but in reality they lie close together forming a smooth surface. This stitch can be worked flat and simply in fine twisted silk or linen thread, or as the Chinese and Japanese employ it, in floss silk finely divided, and with any of these materials makes very dainty decoration. You will have seen somewhere, doubtless, work of this description on some treasured antique garment, a great-great-grandmother's wedding gown, or a gorgeous satin waistcoat of preposterous length, worn in times when dress was stiff and gaudy rather than tasteful, though picturesque for all that. On such garments you may see little flowered borders worked with the utmost refinement and patience in chain or satin stitch, the finest imaginable twisted silk being used, the colours even now both bright and delicate, and chosen of the gayest and most fanciful combinations. Look well at such work when it next comes across your path, and you will see what time, patience and skill can do. To my thinking, satin-stitch is rather clumsy when worked with thick silk or wool. It is obvious that the space to be covered by the needle must not be very broad, for then the characteristic compact and close surface is lost, and the stitches lie loosely in untidy loops ; it will be found inexpedient and awkward to work in short stitches with thick materials, hence it is best to leave this stitch for the finer sorts of work. Another and an effective method of using the stitch consists in first embossing or ' stuffing' the form to be covered, which is done by laying threads of coarse cotton or linen thread backwards and forwards and fastening them down ; and when raised so that the required relief is obtained, the satin-stitch is worked over, at right angles to the direction of the layers of stuffing. For any articles that are expected to receive hard wear this is an excellent and enduring method of work ; but as it is inclined to have a hard and mechanical look (particularly if it is very smoothly done), the relief should be mostly rather flat and low. What I describe here is a comparatively simple form of relief; but presently, in discussing more complicated stitches, I shall have to show that modelling can be elaborated to a very great degree.

Decorative Needlework

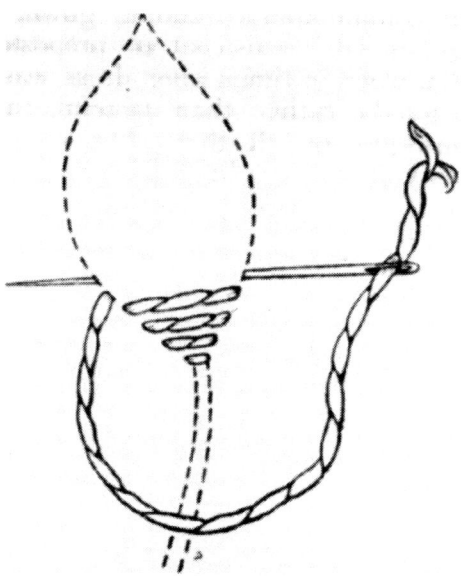

Fig. 6. - Satin Stitch.

Stem-stitch is so simple that it almost explains itself by diagram. One stitch is laid beyond another in a continuous line, which should be smooth and even, the thread being always kept on the same side of the needle. This is essentially adapted to work done in the hand ; it is useful for filling stems and putting in outlines.

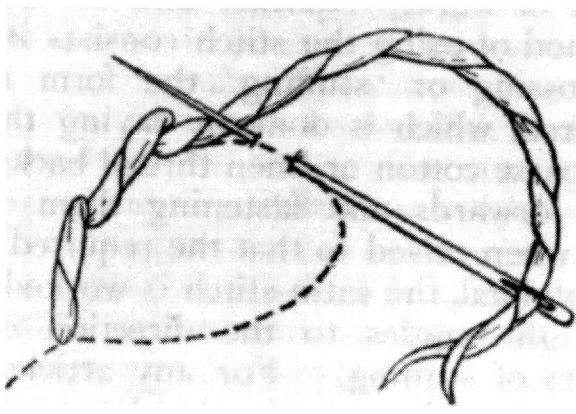

Fig. 7. - Stem Stitch.

Decorative Needlework

Darning can be variously treated, the principle of the stitch being given in Fig. 8, where the threads are shown laid in horizontal lines. (a) The needle is run in and out of the material, following the threads of it, sometimes both right and wrong side alike, and, indeed, resembling the woven stuff. It is used in this way on many of the Eastern embroidered towels that are so much used now. So treated, the stitch has little artistic value in itself, for the same decoration could be obtained with weaving; it is merely a substitute for weaving used for the decoration of their cloths and towels by people who might not care to set up a loom for so slight a purpose.

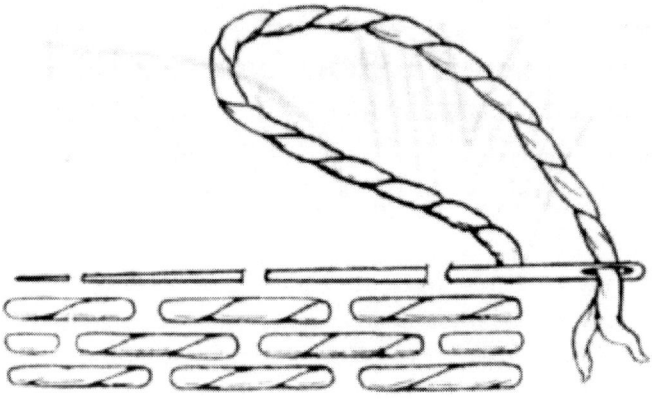

Fig. 8. - Darning.

(b) Another form of darning is, on the contrary, rather elaborate, and involves artistic knowledge in drawing lines and in shading colours. The needle follows the curves and forms of the design, the full stitch only showing on the upper surface of the material. When the design that is being worked is, as is usual, some treatment of flowers and other natural growths, the stitches also radiate outward from a common centre (see Fig. 9). The beginner will encounter several difficulties from the outset, and much more can be learnt by a few hours of personal instruction than by many pages of careful description. When a mass of one colour merely is required, the task is fairly easy, great attention being paid to laying the threads in even lines from centre to edge of the leaf or flower. The stitch, however, is particularly suitable to shading and blending several colours, a skilful worker obtaining both delicacy and variety from this facility.

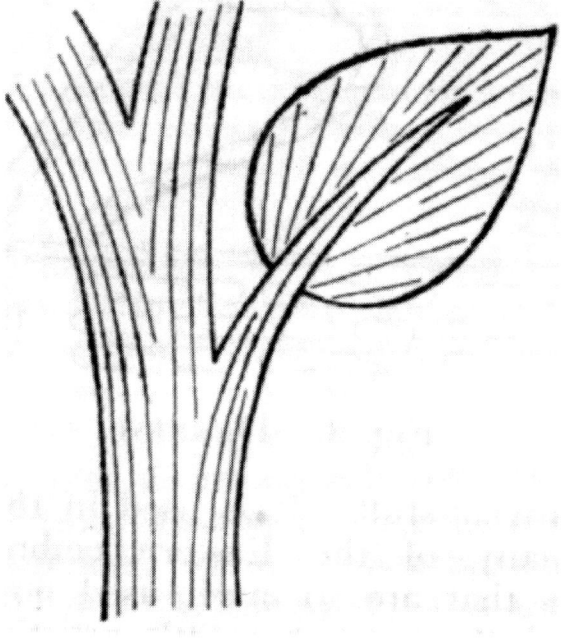

Fig. 9.

But here is our first pause: for this very facility of shading with the needle constitutes in itself a pitfall to the unwary.

It is so tempting to form nice little leaves and flower-petals, all painted up in ' natural' colours almost as good as a picture. But try it. Take a flower on its stem, or spray of leaves, use twenty or thirty different shades of colour to a square foot of work, each leaf executed with its browns, and pinks, and greens, with high light, and lights diffused and reflected, all dragged in by main force, till a libellous caricature of natural growth is achieved ; a caricature having less resemblance to the real thing than the fearless images with a blunt pencil done by a child, whose drawings are symbols of what his eyes see, and have a value all their own as a natural and unaffected expression of natural facts. Then work the same spray in flat and simple colours, say in two shades at most for a leaf, either one side of the leaf light and the other dark, or both sides shaded up from dark to light colour ; flower-petals treated in the same way with very light shading, and with a firm outline to render the pattern clear,

Compare the two methods of work, and a little thought will show you that even to an untrained eye, the latter way of working has a more pleasing look than the former, which is a laborious, pretentious effort to imitate nature in her own colours. A broad and simple style of work should be practised for a long time, and until you have thorough command over colour and composition, and a very sure and definite experience of the value of harmony and contrast and such-like technicalities akin to the painter's art.

Darning, then, is worked in the hand on some loose soft material, and the more yielding the fabric, the quicker the work goes, if that be an advantage. It is not a method of work that will last for ever, the threads all lying on the surface, rather long and loose. Thus it is not suitable for ornamenting surfaces that receive much friction, nor for anything that is easily soiled and has to be constantly refreshed or cleaned. It is a good method for quickly and economically covering large surfaces, but unsuited to important works that are to be durable as well as beautiful.

Another look at Fig. 9, which represents a stem and leaf filled in with work, will show roughly the direction in which the stitches ought to lie. It is absolutely necessary to pay strict attention to this, for correct laying of stitches is one of the first principles of embroidery, and of every sort of needlework, plain or ornamental. The slight radiation of the lines in the leaf falling outwards from a centre should also be noticed. In filling solidly an ornamental form of any breadth, the beginner who ponders over her work will consider how her threads shall be laid so as to fill the space harmoniously, giving at the same time an even texture. She will soon find that the only way to do this is to work from a centre, whence the stitches fall right and left, joining imperceptibly at the top (see Fig. 10), such designs as the embroideress makes use of almost always lending themselves to and suggesting such treatment.

Decorative Needlework

These observations apply equally, of course, to all stitches used for filling solid masses.

The stitches enumerated above are by their nature adapted to soft and supple materials that hang in folds if the size and purpose of the work permit. They are also more suitably done on a material held loose in the hand than stretched in a frame. Those that I shall describe next are stiffer in character, and best done in an embroidery frame ; with some stitches, indeed, one wants both hands at liberty to manipulate the materials, this not being possible when one hand has to be devoted to holding the work.

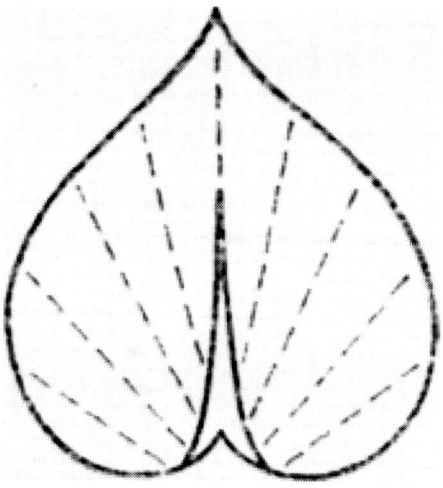

Fig. 10.

Decorative Needlework

Chapter III. Tapestry, Long-and-Short and Feather Stitches

THESE names are somewhat vague, the stitches being merely varieties of the same, but I quote them as the student will constantly hear them spoken of, or come across them in descriptions of old work. Tapestry-stitch, in effect, bears a slight resemblance to woven tapestry (hence its name, I suppose). We must not, however, fall into the common error of calling the art of decorative needlework ' tapestry '; tapestry is a definite technical term for a textile wrought in a loom in a special manner ; and a very ancient art it is too, and a most interesting one.

This stitch is, like darning, used for filling-in broad spaces; but, unlike darning, it is solid back and front (though not identical), and instead of being rather frail and loose, is close and extremely durable. The worker aims at laying the stitches upright in rows (see Fig. 11), and when one row is done the next is laid with the stitches fitting close into those of the last row. This forms a laborious building-up of surface, simple enough where only a little shading or gradation of colour is wanted. Such a method of work was formerly, and is still, a very favourite one for embroidering figures, and here it becomes difficult as well as laborious.

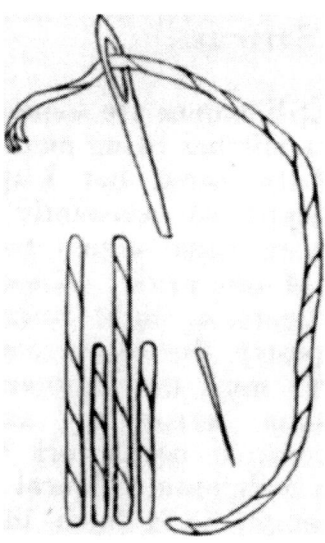

Fig. 11

Decorative Needlework

A faithful study of ancient figure-work, however (and early artists excelled in this branch of the art), will show that the mediaeval needleworker depended greatly on his design, and that he displayed his skill every bit as much in leaving out as in putting in. We find drapery depicted by harmoniously flowing, strongly-marked lines enclosing broad masses of colour ; flesh-tints, which are almost too beautiful and varied for a great painter to reproduce, are frankly and gracefully given up, and our needle artist gives us instead, wellmarked features outlined with a brown or black line, the flesh itself being executed in a sort of monochrome in pinky-brown, with a very little brown shading used where absolutely necessary to mark the expression. Hair, also, is frankly conventionalised, and yet the warm masses and sunlit ringlets of nature are pleasantly interpreted by noble and simple lines and one or two gleams of bright colour. The very simplicity and harmony of such a design give what can never be attained by ill-advised attempts at needle-painting with a hundred different colours, an image of beauty, namely, not marred in the interpretation. It is an.old story - this wisdom of the true artist in thoroughly understanding the capabilities of his materials and tools, and asking no more of his art than it can easily and truthfully give.

It is as well to put down here what I want to say somewhere in these pages with regard to early figure-design: those who are not familiar with the early form of art are apt to laugh at what they consider the childish simplicity with which men and women were portrayed; and, if they are accustomed to ponder over what their eyes see, they will wonder the more, comparing this rude drawing of the figure with the grace and delicacy with which rose and vine tendril, or any such natural growth were drawn.

It is only when the eye becomes accustomed to look for certain qualities in certain arts (not expecting, for instance, to find in an embroidered face transparency of tone or warm depths and shadows as in a picture) that it accepts and appreciates those same qualities, and rejects work that looks more ' real' because it is full of over-confident attempts to realise what is beyond its limited power.

Decorative Needlework

This may sound pedantic; and the student may say that he objects on principle, and as a thinking individual living in the holy nineteenth century, to accepting an oblong with a dot in the middle of it as a drawing of an eye in any art, except that of the child and mud-pie period. He may be right so far as regards modern work -though even here I am not sure; for, as aforesaid, simplicity is one of the first principles of this art. But, although the mediaeval artist's conception of the human figure, characteristic of early times and early beliefs, would certainly be out of keeping with the temper of latter-day design, I still hope that the simplicity and wonderful power of expression of such work will appeal to many, and that few students will turn aside from a genuine admiration of what is admirable herein to jeer at any archaism in feature-drawing. It is one of the great and serious defects of modern criticism in art, not to accept the good faith and beliefs of the period under observation, but to subject every work of past times to a modern test of excellence, which is in itself too often defective.

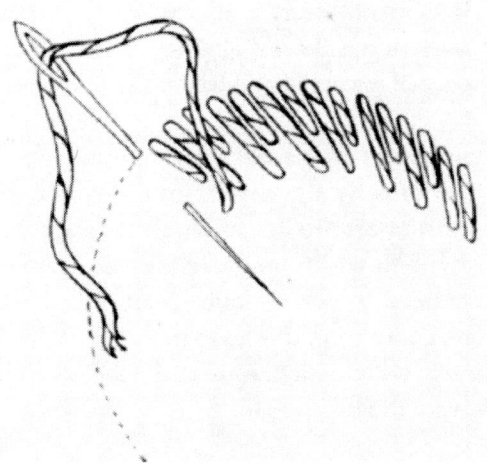

Fig. 12.

I have not forgotten that we are considering a certain group of stitches, the first of which is peculiarly adapted for hangings and panels of a lasting nature, into which figures may be beautifully and effectively introduced. Long-and-short stitch and feather-stitch are merely variants of the same. A glance at the diagram will show that the former is well adapted to filling a broad space, starting from the outline, the stitches radiating slightly from a centre. Another row within this may be added of a different shade, but for the sake of clearness it is not shown here.

In Fig. 13 feather-stitch is shown, the stitches starting from the centre and working outwards. This form of the stitch is constantly employed in old English work of the Jacobean period, and later on into the early eighteenth century. The stitches are built up from a centre line or stem, in close and compact rows, different gradations of colour being used where needed. These slightly varying methods of employing the long-and-short stitches produce extremely thick and enduring work ; I will not say as firm and close in surface as Arras tapestry, but certainly at its finest not far off. The work is usually executed in wool; and, indeed, in silk would necessitate a quite extravagant use of this costly material, which could be better displayed in other ways.

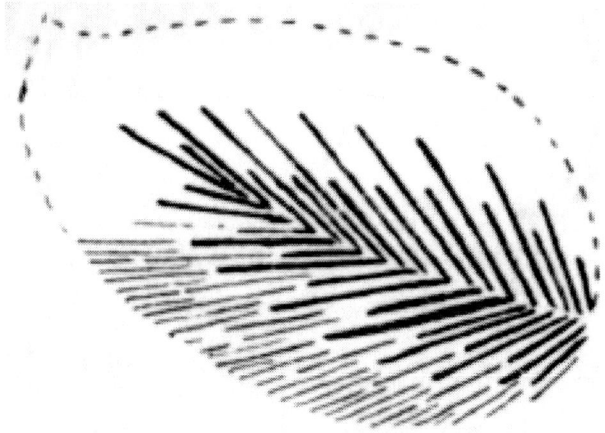

Fig. 13.

In the old work mentioned above, these stitches are sometimes used alone, throughout the whole of an ample hanging; in other specimens they are employed together with other and lighter stitches, often for the sake of filling the surface more rapidly. For instance, in one old hanging that I know, a great bold leaf, about a foot long, is outlined with long-and-short stitch, and the veins done in the kindred feather-stitch ; but the body of the leaf is filled with a crabbed, loose stitch, similar to the looped feather-stitch mentioned in the first chapter. The whole piece of work is a wildly eccentric assembly of different stitches, and has an interesting individuality of its own, for whoever worked it must have taxed her invention to produce variety in a passing spirit of impatience at the monotony or at the dimensions of her work.

Chapter IV. Couching and Applique

THE basis of the many elaborate stitches which would be included under the head of couching is, as the name denotes, a laying down of the threads covering the surface to be filled in. Some writers on the subject limit this name to work executed in gold and silver threads, but I prefer to give it a more general application, as it is often executed in less costly materials. Thus I should include the simple flat laying of threads, either passed down and up through the material or fastened at either end and caught at regular intervals over the surface thus formed (see diagram), and also the raised and moulded work which is built up of various thicknesses of soft linen-thread or of cotton, or sometimes string, and finally covered with closely packed threads of gold ; that is to say, I include the simplest form of this method of work, and the most elaborate. This is a particularly fascinating kind of embroidery, as it allows of much play of colour and invention and variety of stitching. Colour may lie upon colour, and be caught down with spots of yet another shade, and the silks or gold, spread out flat and untwisted, shine and show to their best advantage. A network of one shade of colour over another is often produced by employing this final stitching in various diaper patterns over the loose surface of silk or gold, such effects being often very elaborately worked out. The below diagram (Fig. 14), gives the simplest possible way of using the stitch, and one which is constantly seen in Oriental and Italian hangings of the seventeenth century. The design is filled in by long threads stretching from side to side, either passed underneath and up again, as in satin-stitch, both sides similar, or the needle going down and up again on the same side as close as may be, the silk being thus all on the surface. Next, threads are laid at right angles to the direction of these lines, are also passed from edge to edge, then caught down at regular intervals by little stitches placed alternately so that they form lozenges or squares over the form which is being worked upon. The usual method of laying down the stitches in this form of couching will be seen in Fig. 15. It will be familiar to many who read this in the old and modern Eastern embroidery we see so much of nowadays. In the work alluded to, the filling and the crossing lines

Decorative Needlework

are usually all wrought with the same colour. The surface thus produced is admirable in its shining texture, but one feels the want here and there of a little more play of colour, to which all these couching stitches are, as aforesaid, particularly adapted.'

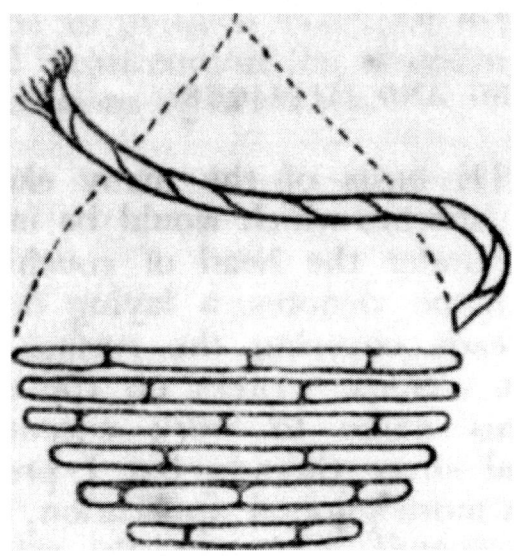

Fig. 14. - Flat Couching.

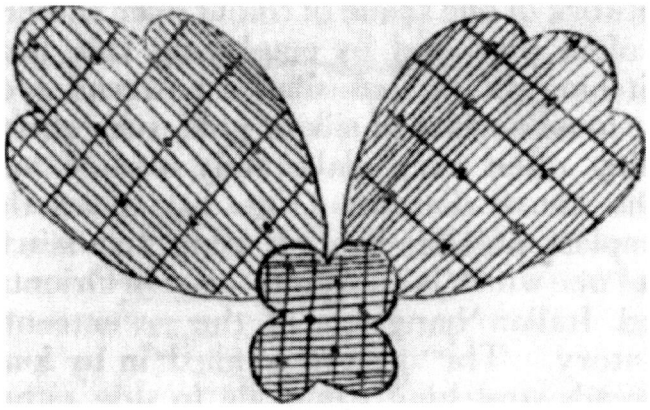

Fig. 15.

Decorative Needlework

So far our work is very simple, though care and attention will be needed to keep the threads beautifully flat, and, if floss-silk is used, to keep even the suspicion of a twist from it; care also in laying the crossing threads at moderately even distances. Variety can also be made by crossing the threads lattice-wise, first one way and then the other, and catching them down with any little stitches that occur to the worker. But the next stage of elaboration will require more skill and attention, and, being more valuable artistically, will repay the extra trouble taken. Instead of covering the design with threads laid directly on the ground, it (the design) is stuffed or raised to a certain height by one or two or more layers of linen thread loosely caught down at intervals, or even by cotton wool, which would then, however, have to be covered with a thin muslin to keep it neat; the work thus prepared is then covered with its final layer of silk or gold thread or what not. This moulded and raised work is best adapted for applique work, which is cut and ' applied ' to another ground, of which more anon. It is a rather stiff and formal method of work, unless done on a large scale for bold decoration to be seen at a distance. If executed on a small scale, the materials should be chosen very fine and pliable, and the work itself be extremely minute and raised ; for we never get with couched work that graceful flow and sweep of one stitch on another which those methods give us in which the needle follows the curve and swing of the design. The characteristics of couching lie chiefly in richness of invention in the stitching, and in beautiful colour and materials. The diagram (Fig. 16) will show how the stuffing threads lie, with the sharply marked lines for indicating the veins sewn on over them. These, again, are hidden by the threads of silk or gold, which must always be laid at right angles to the direction of the last layer of stuffing. The veins can be clearly defined by a line of stitches either side, or can be left merely indicated in the course of sewing down, which will be enough if the vein line be well accentuated.

Decorative Needlework

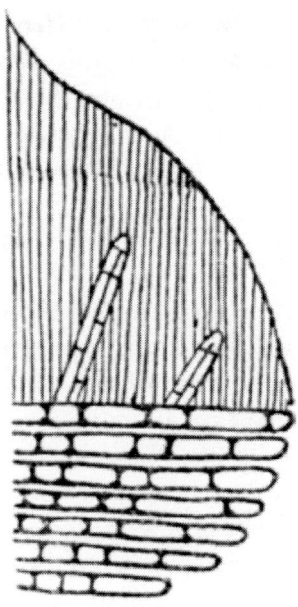

Fig. 16. - Raised Couching.

This sufficiently characteristic method of couching' will be guidance for other varieties, and it will be borne in mind that ' gold couching ' is no special stitch which has to be learnt anew, but simply couching as described here, worked with gold thread and cord, and only far more difficult to master because of the stubborn nature of the gold itself. There is some very pretty work of the sixteenth century (Italian), in which the ground is couched in long lines, the leaves also couched flat, the flowers worked in tapestry stitch following the curves of the design, but outlined with a very thick, close, raised thread, which carries out the stiff character of the couching. The stems are in raised work, and some shields with the arms of the owners of the work are introduced in very thick raised gold, heraldry having been always a favourite form of decoration in needlework.

Precious stones, most frequently seed pearls, are often used in rich couched work. I have recently seen a very pretty richly-designed and richly-worked glove that once belonged to Henry VIII., on which are portrayed the lion, the rose, and the crown. The lion, a harmless and amiable looking animal, though drawn as rampant along the wrist of the glove, is thickly wrought in gold, with a pearl eye, if my memory serves me. The crowns are also gold, and the roses highly embossed and laid thickly over with a multitude of fine seed pearls. There is a little old book with an embroidered cover in one of the museums wherein is inserted in the place of honour in the middle of the front board a large flat garnet or ruby. The work is further enriched by gold and pearls, but the isolation of this pale pink stone gives quite a peculiar value to the bit of needlework. This is all by the way, however, and I do not advise learners to tamper at all with pearls and stones until they feel that they have reached a stage of excellence which renders their work capable of bearing the weight and accentuation that such a striking addition gives to needlework. Poor work thus adorned looks yet poorer, and is pretentious to no purpose.

It must be remembered that these and other couched stitches, as well as applique, are all admirably suited for decorating materials which are to be displayed flat ; and that for any textiles which are destined to hang loosely in folds such work is impracticable, unless, indeed, it is laid on as a powdered pattern, scattered at intervals over the surface of the cloth. For small objects on which, owing to their size, much work can be lavished, and which usually need to be enduring and firm, the stiffer forms of couching are peculiarly suitable. It wears well, and gives scope for great ingenuity and variety; without which, I need hardly say, a small piece of work becomes insignificant, and merely a toy of fashion for the moment.

I include under the name of applique, or 'applied' work, every sort of embroidery which, being worked solidly on one material, is then cut out and laid down upon another, and secured by various ornamental stitches. This is rather a rough-and-ready definition, and requires amplification. Suppose, for instance, that a certain material is to be ornamented by having a group of flowers repeated over the surface at regular intervals. The group of flowers, or what not, is worked on some stout ground, such as holland or coarse linen; when finished so far, the work is cut out carefully, the scissors following round the edge of the work about a quarter of an inch or half an inch away, according to the size and nature of the work ; the work is then laid upon the ground material, which is ready stretched in a frame. When a spray is well in its place, care being taken that every leaf shall be duly laid and no curve pulled the least out of shape, the raw edges are secured by firm stitches, and the whole design is edged with a gold thread, or a twist of silk or wool, or with a gimp or braid, according to the nature of the materials which are being dealt with. This method of work is, in fact, considerably modified by the materials employed. For a great bold wall-hanging in wools on serge we should not show the same nicety of finish that would be required for a delicate piece of work in fine silk and gold thread, to be laid on a choice bit of satin. In the former, the cut edges would be covered by the broad gimp or cord surrounding the design, whereas in the finer work the edges, wherever possible, must be dexterously tucked away underneath ; for the slim outline will not hide any uneven-ness here, and nothing looks so clumsy and ugly as a thick outline too heavy for the design. This turning-in of edges and sewing down very neatly is the most troublesome part of the work, and requires deft fingers ; one has to be careful not to cut too near the work, nor too deep into the corners ; but the broader the margin left, the more tiresome it is to turn in neatly, especially if the design is small or the least bit intricate. The design for such work should be of the simplest and broadest; leaves should have a simple outline, or if serrated the serrations can be shown by two or three little stitches within the outline. Compare, for instance, Fig. 17 and Fig. 18, in which two different forms of design are shown, the one, as I take it, suitable for this work, and the other unsuited to it. In Fig. 17 a conventionalised bud and leaf are drawn simply and even crudely, but drawn in a way that suffices for our purpose. In Fig. 18, on the other hand, a chrysanthemum with its deeply serrated leaf is drawn, also conventionalised. There would be nothing elaborate or troublesome in this if worked in some stitches ; but in the form of work we are treating of now it would be almost impossible to do neatly, and I do not believe in trying to conquer impossibilities when there is a straight and simple way of doing what we want. Now, the very fact that broad and simple forms are a sine qua non in this method, makes the work very well adapted for decoration that is intended to catch the eye at a distance ; but for richer work to be admired and

Decorative Needlework

handled more elaboration will be wanted in finishing. Flourishes and tendrils can be added, or a whole back-ground pattern introduced behind the solid applique groups. This sort of ' tracery ' seems to give a coherence to the heavier parts of the design, and is very helpful in enriching and lightening it.

Fig. 17. - Suitable for Applique.

Applique is not a stitch or series of stitches, but a certain method of work, irrespective of the stitches employed therein. But certain stitches are more adapted than others for working the groups and sprays to be applied. The more solid stitches will, of course, be used, and the various sorts of raised couching, especially gold couching, are perhaps the best for this purpose, and the stiffer worked the better. Botticelli, the Florentine artist, is said by his historian, Vasari, to have been specially fond of this work, and to have made designs for it. Vasari, indeed, said that he invented it, but I suspect this of being a flight of the historian's imagination, which was lively at times, and not likely to err on the side of understating the case.

Decorative Needlework

Fig. 18. - Unsuitable for Applique.

A simple form of applied work that is far from costly so far as concerns time and material, and yet effective, consists of cutting out shapes in coloured cloth or silk, and laying them directly on the material to be ornamented, and then connecting the whole with outlines and what veining and marking of leaf and so forth the design seems to require for its completion. Even this simple work should be put into an embroidery frame ; it is so much easier to manipulate the work when both hands are at liberty.

Chapter V. Patchwork and Quilting

THE laying down of one stuff on another for decorative purposes brings me to the mention of patchwork, a time-honoured kind of stitchery, familiar by name at least to all of us. More time-honoured, indeed, than one would think, for the patchwork quilts which form a charming and pathetic record of our grandmothers' girlhood and courtship, where we affectionately admire the little scraps of brocade ' worn the first night I danced with your dear grandfather,' are but a survival of, or speaking more strictly, a variation from, a different sort of patchwork done in very far-off times in distant Egypt, that land where the arts of life were flourishing exuberantly long before history even begins for us of the Western world. Patchwork is formed by piecing together bits of stuff of chosen texture and colour, cut in various shapes and neatly stitched together ; if the shapes are at all complex, the fitting has to be most precisely and accurately managed, and forms the only really troublesome process of this sort of needlework.

In its simple form such work is easy enough, but in the East it has been, and is still, elaborately carried out, with intricate design and beautiful colour. It is rather difficult to give a clear idea of this curious embroidery by mere description. You must imagine a mosaic, as it were, but instead of being made up of bits of marble or of coloured glass, this mosaic is formed of pieces of stuff of different colours, fitted together into certain ornamental shapes and finished with touches of colour in embroidery stitches. Such patchwork distinctly comes into the category of things artistic: while the quilts and such-like of the last and the present centuries are only pretty pieces of neat stitchery, in which an elementary sense of geometric design and colour yet remains in the sometimes-clever arrangement of the different scraps of dress stuff of which they are composed.

Quilting is done in different ways, but generally speaking, it consists of placing a thin layer of some soft yielding material, such as cotton-wool, between the ground to be worked on (be it thin silk, or fine cotton, or linen) and a thin lining ; the design is then worked in firm

Decorative Needlework

stitches, taken right through to the reverse side. The result is a slight relief, which gives a pleasant effect. A cord is sometimes laid between the two surfaces, and stitched down either side, making a higher relief. Quilting can be varied considerably, but this description will, I think, be enough to enable the student to identify any different forms of quilting that she may come across among old or modern work.

Gold and Silver Thread – It is usual to introduce metal threads in the more elaborate kinds of needlework; some work, indeed, consisting entirely of gold. But solid gold-work requires careful treatment lest it become vulgarised, as it does notably in some bad work of a late period. I have said enough about it in Chapter IV (Couching and Applique). to intimate that its use requires a special knowledge and dexterity, as it is difficult to handle, owing to its want of flexibility. For all practical purposes there are two kinds of thread now in general use, (1) paper-gold and (2) tinsel-gold. (1.) The paper-gold, which comes to us principally, if not entirely, from Japan, and is a great favourite now, consists of gilded strips of very fine tough paper, such as the Japanese have the great art of making, wound round a silken thread. It does not tarnish, which is, of course, a great advantage. (2) Tinsel-gold is very much more brilliant and is made by the metal being wire-drawn into a fine thread, which is wound round coloured silk. Being really silver, gilded more or less thickly, it tarnishes readily in proportion to the quality of the gilding, which determines the value of the thread produced. Otherwise it is pleasant to use, and is a good firm material for solid work, with its brilliance a little softened by appropriate colours. I give its technical name, not knowing how else to call it; but the word 'tinsel,' gives a false impression of the quality of this beautiful material, which must by no means be classed along with the tin-foil splendours which delight our eyes at the pantomime on Boxing Night. However, much beautiful and fine work can be done with the paper-gold ; and the ancient form of it, gilded vellum, namely, very thin and finely cut into strips, and wound round a thread, was universally used in the most flourishing times of the arts of figured stuff-weaving and embroidery. This, and the flat beaten gold, forming a sort of gold ribbon, were certainly the forms of gold most used in ancient times ;

but ' it were enquiring too curiously' to enter here into the history of the use of gold and silver in textiles and embroideries, although it is so interesting a subject of research that one is almost tempted to do so. The first development of wire-drawn gold would certainly be from the delicate manipulation of flat gold ribbon, rolling it with the hand into a fragile wire, a lengthy and difficult operation, but surprisingly finely done in the earliest times when machinery was not. For indeed, though people talk about the wonders of machinery, the patience and dexterity of man's handiwork without the help of any machine is far more wonderful.

I must repeat that gold and silver are usually treated in some firm and stiff manner in various couching stitches. It is at once the most effective and the easiest way of using these beautiful materials, but skilful workers will introduce gold into lighter needlework, threading and passing it back and forth like a thread of silk, Gold and silver so treated can be seen in the muslin towels and cloths that come over here from India, and from Turkey and Bulgaria. The gold is passed through the thin stuff, of sometimes gossamer texture, with wonderful smoothness and precision, and in its way, nothing daintier can be imagined than this rich and heavy decoration shining among the floating folds of a light and delicate muslin. In couched gold the metal is usually threaded in a large-eyed needle, and occasionally passed through the ground, but it has to be very carefully laid down with minute stitches of fine silk of different colours. Silver thread is sometimes used also, but the rapidity with which it tarnishes proves a great drawback; which is a pity, as it is almost as beautiful as the gold. The reader can refer to what I have written about couching, which equally applies to gold-work when used in this way; though with all the difference between a pliable and a stubborn material. I should always advise learners, ambitious of excelling herein, to get some special instruction in gold and silver needlework, as a little teaching by word of mouth would soon dispel difficulties that appear to be very discouraging at first.

Chapter VI. Setting to Work

MOST people are familiar with the aspect of an embroidery-frame, or have some idea of what it is like. It consists of two 'beams' or rollers (A) on which the textile is wound, or to which it is merely attached by being sewn to a piece of stout webbing nailed to the wood, and two cross-sticks (B) which complete the frame and do the stretching, transversely by threads passed through the material to be worked on, and lengthways by means of pegs or screws in the beams. This is the ancient loom, simple and primitive, and coeval with any sort of textile first woven by the sons of Adam: two upright posts stuck in the ground, and a beam above to hold the warp-threads, and weights below to keep all tight, or a second beam to hold the finished web. Instead of working the needle in and out of the woven stuff, the weaver works his shuttle in and out of the warp-threads, forming the web or woven stuff itself; or, when the simple machine is a little elaborated, shoots the shuttle between the two sets of threads, which are kept apart by a simple contrivance. The old hand-loom can be seen figured in many of the mediaeval manuscripts, where ladies are drawn carding, spinning, weaving, and embroidering, sitting in pretty gardens, the blue sky overhead, with garlands or jewels in their hair, and graceful gowns on their bodies - a different picture from that presented by our latter-day weaving-sheds, where every hour spent in the hot exhausted air among the clatter and crash of machinery is an undeserved penance to the work-girls.

Our embroidery-frame is either supported on a table or against a chair ; or, which is far more convenient, is set in a stand on the ground, an arrangement which steadies the work, and leaves both hands free to ply the needle. In preparing and stretching framework great neatness and precision should be observed from the outset. The first little piece of carelessness is demoralising, and leads to more; and, indeed, mistakes and disasters to the work may arise from not straining it carefully in the frame, quite straight and exact, the raw edges cut even and hemmed or sewn to a stout tape, through which to pass the strings that are used to stretch the work.

Decorative Needlework

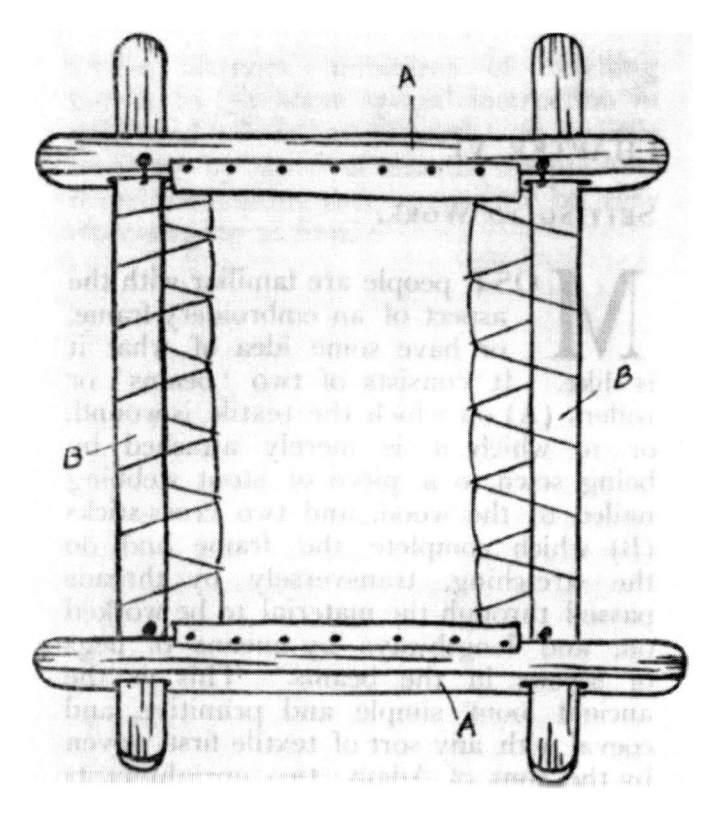

Fig. 19.

Everything must be kept very clean (it is impossible to be too particular in this respect), and a thin cheap lining-muslin should be procured to sew over the parts of the work which are finished or not yet started. The learner will soon notice that if she gets into a careful, precise method from the first, the difficulties of working will the more readily be minimised, Silks, too, must be carefully kept, the different shades of one colour arranged together, the colours being labelled for working at night, until the worker is well practised in recognising the different shades by artificial light. Gold and silver should be kept from the light as much as possible, and should be cut off in lengths not over long, as the metal thread easily spoils and breaks. Floss-silk will want much nicety in keeping, as well as in handling, for it gets rough in a little while, not being twisted, or only very slightly. Of such silks none should be left lying about but what is needed for present use, which must be wound neatly on cards, if not on nice little ivory or mother-of-pearl winders, which are certainly a luxury, but good to have, as they are smooth and clean, and keep the silk fresh.

These observations are not so trivial as perhaps they seem, and all tend towards the one general axiom, ' Cleanliness and neatness,' without which your work will be naught. I have sometimes seen work, which was allowed to lie about the room between-whiles, gathering all the impurities of smoke and dust; the general dimness of aspect of such work can be imagined, and shows in itself bad workmanship. True talent, like true genius, is never slovenly ; for the acquiring of this quality of order and care, on which I lay so much stress, is part of the apprenticeship that every worker with hand and eye must go through, be it in workshop or studio, or labouring alone and self-taught, towards excellence in any art.

A few words more about setting to work before we pass on to consider design and the nature of materials used in embroidery. I have said elsewhere that, in arranging and starting a piece of work, you must consider whether the stitches employed will necessitate the use of a frame, and also what stitches will look well in unison. Some stitches are more quickly and better done in the hand; and as it is certainly-tiring to sit a long while bending over a frame, even to those who are used to it, it is well to avoid the use of one for work that can be done without it.

For instance, satin stitch is often worked in a frame ; but when worked on ordinary materials that are not very fine or likely to pucker, it is equally well done, and much more quickly, without stretching. For darning, and for chain-stitch and other looped stitches, I consider a frame out of the question. When chain-stitch is worked on a stretched material it is done with a hooked needle, and called tambour work. Tapestry, long and short, and featherstitches are practically all stitches for the frame; as also, it goes almost without saying, are couching, applique, and similar methods of work. The rough division of stitches into frame-work and non-framework is a kind of guide as to what stitches to use together. But the learner will do well to avoid a heterogeneous mixture of stitches and had best confine herself to the use of one or two. Variety and effect are more honestly produced by good design and careful colouring than by the skilfullest admixture of stitches.

Chapter VII. Design, Convention and Realism

THE most important element in successful work is the choice of design, and I shall therefore be obliged to linger a little over this subject, as it is impossible to make a clear explanation to those of my readers to whom the subject may be entirely strange without a good deal of enlargement of general axioms. While inferior work can be tolerated for the sake of the design, if that is good (though the two rarely go together), excellent work on a worthless design must be cast aside as labour lost; so that, you see, design is the very soul and essence of beautiful embroidery, as it is of every other art, exalted or humble. It is enough to break one's heart to see the labour and skill sometimes spent over would-be decorative ornament, that instead of being full of beauty and intention, is more like a heterogeneous collection of unmeaning shapes, lacking form, which the designer himself, if put to it, could as ill explain as anyone else.

Having said this much, I must here say what I mean by design worthy to be wedded to good work. First we must consider the nature of Design generally and ask, for instance (a) Why the otherwise blank surface of the wall of my study is decorated by a patterned paper; and (b) Why this particular paper is chosen of willow-boughs rather than roses or honeysuckles, or any other growth ? (a) In the first place, it is one of man's instincts to beautify his life by whatever means are in his power, and a wall-paper printed in colours with some ornamental form is more pleasing in his sight (as a make-shift, be it said, for handsomer decoration, such as wood panelling or woven hangings) than the bare blank surface of plain white or colour. This is the instinctive pleasure in life (the 'joie de vivre' in the comprehensive sense), which makes life desirable, but which is too often restrained or even altogether crushed out of us by external circumstance, (b) Again, the ornamented surface takes the shape of willow-boughs on account of my own especial fancy for them, and the pleasant river-scenes they recall; this constitutes the personal element of taste or fancy, and it is this individuality which divides what is called ' original' work from that which is wanting in character and vigour ; in a word, lifeless. Thus we have the instinct, and the more or less developed capacity of man to adorn his life, on the one hand; and on the other, the individual taste which directs that capacity on to this, that, or the other lines: Design embodying these two elements, universal and individual.

The application of decorative design in connection with the minor arts or handicrafts, as they are called, will obviously be for the adornment of articles of daily and of especial use. Every commonest article of every-day use shows the remains (machine-made now, of course) of what was once put on by hand in the course of making the article, by way of decoration, such as the rim of blue or pink colour round the edge of a penny plate, or the star at the bottom of a beer-house tumbler.

As in embroidery we have only to do with decorative design applied to flat surfaces, and especially to textiles, I must, in so large and interesting a subject, limit myself to this particular branch. Given a certain space, the aim of the designer is to lay on it ornament, first, pleasing to the eye, and next, suitable to the materials in hand, and to the future use of the article when finished. For the present we only have to deal with the former pleasure-giving quality. Now, the modern tendency (a reaction, doubtless, from the Renaissance conventionality which has so long held its ground) is to copy some spray or bough directly from nature, and to lay it down haphazard on the surface to be ornamented; a few stray petals or a broken leaf and a caterpillar being peppered about elsewhere without rhyme or reason ; this is then called a ' quaint' design. When I tell you that symmetry, order, and balance are above all things essential, and that no attempted copying of the painter's art (for that is what it amounts to) in such dissimilar and insufficient materials is permissible, you will understand that the 'quaint' design is wrong in the very nature of it. The given space must be filled by forms in certain rhythmical sequence, which may either be masked or plainly marked.

In designing for reproduction by mechanical means the various forms are arranged so as to be repeated in regular order; but for our purpose, repetition of a design should be sparingly resorted to, and principally for large surfaces ; for the great charm of embroidery lies in its richness and diversity of invention, within certain well-understood limits.

You will have often heard the words convention and conventional used as opposed to naturalistic forms in a decorative design. Now, the first thing the designer will do is to go to natural growths and animal life, and show his pleasure in them by studying their infinite variety and beauty, and introducing them into his work. These studies should be constantly and faithfully made, until the artist has familiarised himself with all possible peculiarities and diversities of such things. But his own work should merely recall nature, not absolutely copy it; the living flower should inspire a living ornament in his brain, certain characteristics being dwelt upon, but the forms all simplified, leaves flatly arranged, stems bent into flowing curves to fill the required spaces.

Whatever growth is chosen as a model will thus be re-presented by the draughtsman's hand, but translated, as it were, and serving the purpose of giving delight almost as well as when growing in the fields: in exchange for the subtle, unconscious and untranslatable beauty of nature, we get the charm of conscious art; the artist exacting service from nature, and obtaining it, graciously and ungrudgingly given just in so far as it is lovingly and frankly asked for. Here is (Fig. 20) a sketch of a rose-bud, conventionalised a great deal, as you will notice ; as a likeness of the rose-bud it is too rough to be worth much, but quite sufficiently recalls the real thing for the purposes of needlework. It was not drawn without careful consideration of a live rose-bud, all the little nicks in whose leaves, and twirls of whose tendrils were admiringly noted, but not reproduced in this sketch.

Thus much of Convention, then, as an essential of decorative design. Next I would ask you, when you have a design for flat decoration in your hands, or are yourself designing, to consider carefully whether it fulfils its first purpose of well and symmetrically covering a certain defined space ? If this space is not so filled, the would-be design must be rejected as not fulfilling its function. The following sketches (Figs. 21 and 22) may roughly supplement this. Given a square space to be ornamented simply, two ways of doing so are shown ; In the one (Fig. 21) a spray is 'gracefully and negligently,' as a fashion-paper would say, laid in one corner, a leaf or two stuck on somewhere else, no matter where. The spray is inoffensive in itself, but however beautifully and carefully it might be drawn, there is no form or symmetry in the grouping; in fact, no thought. Next we have a square (Fig. 22) with rosettes at the four corners, little spots running along the edge forming a border, and a circle in the middle, with more spots round it, forming a centre rosette. The whole is a mere grouping of spots big and little, symmetrically arranged, simply, but sufficiently decorative, when compared with Fig. 21.

Fig. 20.

Decorative Needlework

Fig. 21.

Fig. 22.

Decorative Needlework

However, having warned you against the dangers of so-called 'naturalism,' I must point out that conventionalism in the extreme brings us to an equally unsatisfactory result; that is, when natural objects are so changed as to become either grotesque or meaningless. In fact, a 'conventional' design in common talk means something of this sort; that is, form which has now no true relation to natural growth. It would be of service to us here, as an illustration, if we could compare the convention of, say, the design of a fourteenth century embroidered cope (of no more than ordinary beauty, but good of its style) with the design of some late Renaissance quilt or hanging, or what not.

In the earlier work we have the convention which compels natural objects into a certain subjection without losing sight of their character, and without robbing them of their grace. In the later work - and I am careful to speak of late Renaissance, as the early style has a beauty and delicacy all its own - we have the convention which has forgotten all about nature, or thinks to improve upon it, spinning ideas out of itself like a silkworm. It is almost unnecessary to say that with this exhaustive method the supply of ideas soon gives out, and we have strange and extravagant forms, at once luxuriant and weak in line, and poor in fancy - conventional indeed, and nothing besides.

The deduction from this is, therefore, not to draw a line you do not understand and cannot explain to yourself. Be definite before everything - let every form you put on paper be something, explain something.

Some of the natural forms most dear to the designer as models are so intricate that the explanatory and strictly conventional method is the only method of representing them at all. Look, for instance, at the numerous drawings by the ancient Egyptian artists of papyrus beds, executed with extreme simplicity, and almost amounting to mere shorthand notes of the real thing, but none the less beautiful in their way.

Chapter VIII. Contrast and Repetition

TO get a harmonious design we must study and consider well of what qualities such a design should be built up. The subordination of one form to another in some way is essential ; there must be some leading lines and forms, that, from their central position or broader massing, attract the eye more than others. In the sprig (Fig. 23), which composes the powdered pattern indicated in Fig 24, the flower is the central point of attraction, the leaves and stems being subordinate to it. The forms of which a design is made should fall into their places naturally and without effort. On looking at some unskilful decorative work, every line seems to clash with another, the design being restless, and 'all on end,' lacking that breadth and repose which characterises good work. The danger of insipidity and dulness that a 'quiet'design may fall into must be avoided by contrast, the subordination of one part to another, spoken of above. Such contrast may be obtained in various ways ; for instance, by opposing delicate tracery or smaller forms to the principal masses of striking or broad forms, such opposition presenting a rich and pleasing variety to the eye. This contrast implies a certain complexity of design, which is not always necessary or suitable, but it certainly greatly enhances the richness of the intended decoration.

Fig. 23.

Decorative Needlework

After thinking over this point, and writing thus far, I turned to Ruskin's 'Elements of Drawing' to see what his word to the beginner is on the subject of Composition and Design. I find here said so exactly what is wanted on many points, that I hope those who wish to pursue the subject will look up this volume, which contains much food for thought throughout its pages. Many of the observations apply as much to the decorative as to the higher pictorial arts, and I am tempted to quote the master's words on the 'Law of Contrast,' which, giving as they do the true ethical meaning of this law in a few clear and simple words, should be helpful to you. He says: 'Of course the character of everything is best manifested by Contrast. Rest can only be enjoyed after labour ; sound, to be heard clearly, must rise out of silence; light is exhibited by darkness, darkness by light; and so on in all things. Now in art every colour has an opponent colour, which, if brought near it, will relieve it more completely than any other ; so, also, every form and line may be made more striking to the eye by an opponent form or line near them ; a curved line is set off by a straight one, a massive form by a slight one, and so on ; and in all good work nearly double the value, which any given colour or form would have uncombined, is given to each by contrast.' The next paragraph contains a warning against vulgar exaggeration in the use of this artifice.

The value of repetition in decoration on large surfaces will easily be seen, but it is further needed in the different parts of the design itself, as, for instance, the repetition of petal against petal, leaf beside leaf. Symmetry goes hand in hand with this, leaf balancing leaf on the opposite sides of the stem. There is also that more subtle repetition found in elaborate design, of one form 'echoing' another, without exactly repeating it. This, however, will be better understood after studying good ornamental work closely, and carefully considering its composition.

A glance at the diagram (Fig. 24) will give some idea of the nature of these laws of repetition, balance, and so forth, that govern design. The diagram represents the simplest possible expression of a 'powdered pattern,' that is, of a design dotted or powdered over the surface at regular intervals. In the little sprigs we have repetition,

Decorative Needlework

and in so far as they alternate in position in alternate rows we have symmetry, and symmetry and balance also in the individual sprig, the leaves of which lie opposed each side of the stem ; in the rosettes or groups of dots between the sprigs, as well as in the construction of the sprigs themselves, we have contrast or subordination.

Fig. 24.

I have sufficiently enlarged elsewhere on Convention and Realism, or truth to nature ; I will therefore only again remind you, and very earnestly, not to note carelessly one-half of my observations on this important point without due consideration of the other half, the one assertion being incomplete without the other. Man's instinct is creative as much as imitative, and the very convention he adopts, determined by his own personality, is nothing but a re-presentation based on observation of and fidelity to nature.

Decorative Needlework

Chapter IX. Lines and Curves

IN considering the different elements of Design, a little talk about the value and qualities of lines will clear up a good many difficulties for the beginner. Remember well this : a beautiful curve has variety in every inch of it ; that is to say, it changes its direction constantly. Look at Fig. 25, which at A shows a curve which is the segment of a circle. A true circle being drawn mechanically with a compass from a fixed centre, every portion of its line is regular and equal in value to every other portion. Such a curve in its mechanical perfection, therefore, is unsatisfactory to the designer's eye, and its unconscious, as well as conscious, adoption should be vigilantly guarded against. At B, on the contrary, we have a pleasing curve, very familiar to anyone who notes the poise of a flower-stem or the swing of a tree-branch. Look at it and compare it with A, and you will see what is meant by variety in a curve, at C, the outline of a full spring-bud, we have a still more varied line.

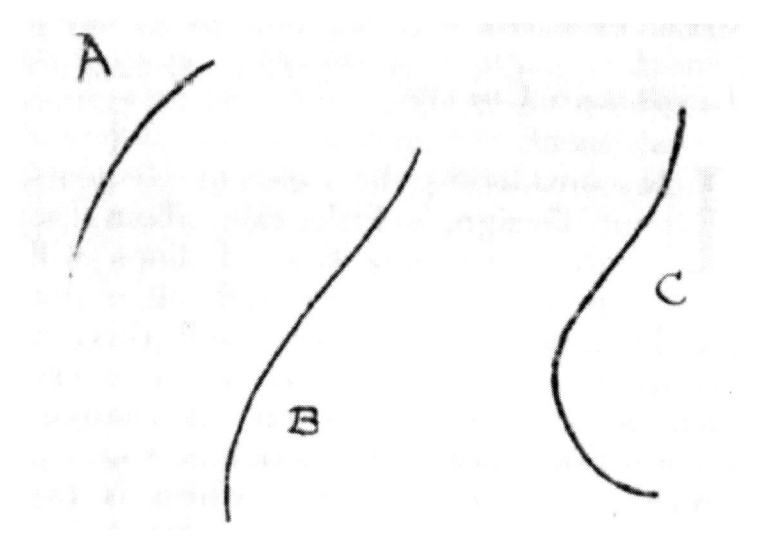

Fig. 25.

Nothing could be better as studies for simple and complex curves than careful copying of a single leaf from each of the different plants and trees which may be accessible to you. Note the difference between the exquisite crispness of outline in the beech-leaf and the delicate simplicity of the slim willow-leaf; or again, the rich variety of line in the serrated vine-leaf. There is another thing to remember about curves : every curved line is stronger at its base or attachment than at its apex ; the further from the base, the more delicate, and finally the more weak it grows. A curve, therefore, which is prolonged beyond a certain point loses its strength, its expression of poising and balance, and the indecision that results is extremely unpleasing. In Fig. 26 curve A is right ; continue it a little, and we get B, which reminds one of the woefully weak lines of a bad wall-paper. If a prolonged curve is wanted for some definite purpose, it should contain an actual repetition of direction as at C.

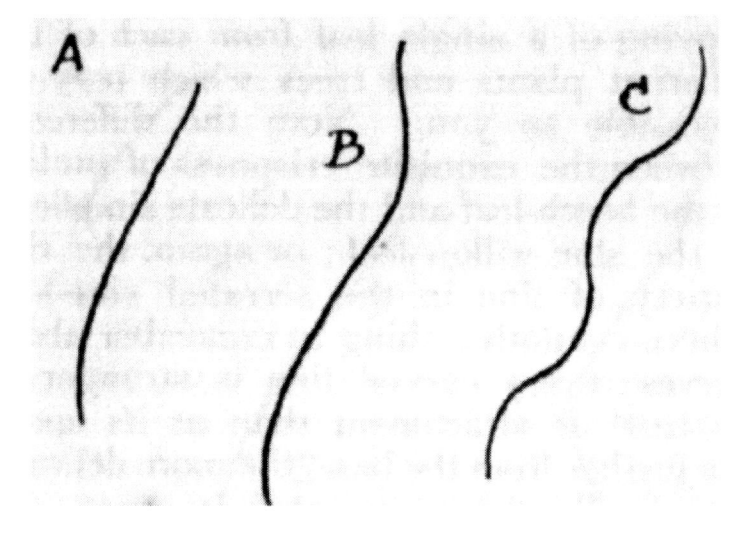

Fig. 26.

In planning out and starting a design, always work from a centre, both for the detail and in the composition itself. For instance, if you are bringing a rose into your work, fix in your eye a certain central point, and let the petals converge towards it; the same in drawing a leaf (such a complex leaf as at B, Fig. 27). Without some such definite order the petals of the flower, or the parts of the leaf, will lie at all sorts of odd angles, and you will be puzzled, and unable to tell exactly where and how they are wrong.

Designs differ considerably in form and method: some are worked entirely from a centre, while others are more flowing, and may have a central form, but not set or strongly marked. But in all ornamental design, whatever the construction, the details themselves must have this definite centre, which gives unity and coherence, be it masked or revealed. The law of radiation is, in fact, all-pervading in design. In the little branch (A), in the diagram, the stem itself, roughly speaking, constitutes the centre, whence the leafstalks radiate and fall outwards with just that amount of irregularity, or, more strictly speaking (for nothing is wholly irregular in design), that amount of variation that will be felt and made use of as the student grows more familiar with the designers art.

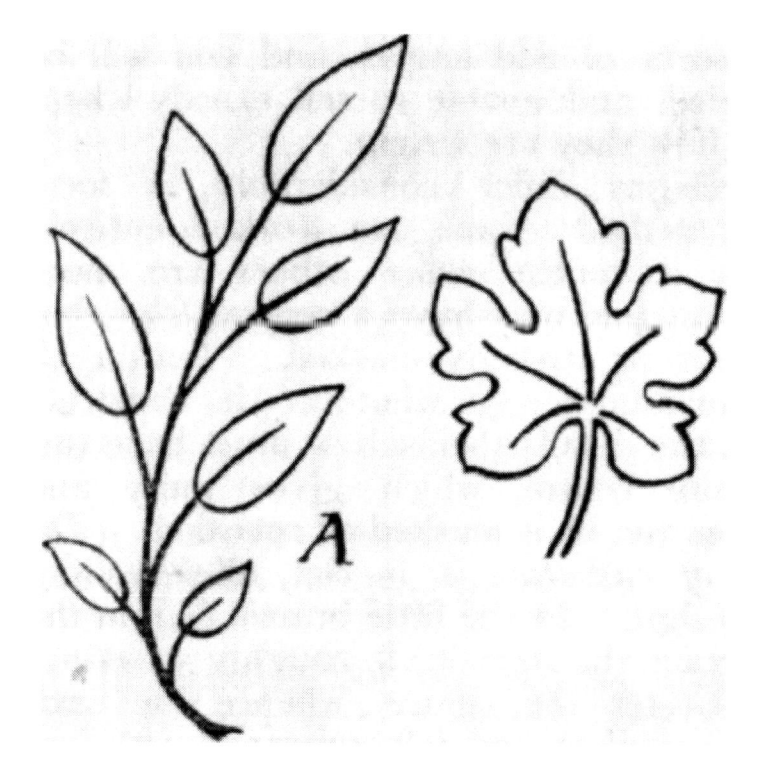

Fig. 27.

I think with these notes on the formation of design, the student should now have some inkling as to what to study among the examples of fine ornament in our museums, or from coloured plates of the same, which can be easily obtained. It will be easier now, I hope, to recognise the qualities, good or bad, of such work, and from study to practice should be but a short step.

In always recommending ancient rather than modern work for study, I do so with intent; for, in mediaeval ornament, whether in an illuminated manuscript or a figured stuff, or embroidered cloth, one is always sure that though the interest of detail and beauty of form may vary very much, the work is not lacking in the essential qualities of good design, and is thorough in its way, and executed with due knowledge of material and with due skill of hand. In modern decorative work the estrangement between designer and executant generally creates a want of unity and coherence in the work produced. On the one hand, the designer frequently has no full knowledge of the materials and tools employed, and his drawings, made independently of such things, lose force or delicacy in the execution ; while on the other hand, the craftsman loses the knowledge he formerly possessed of the value of lines and masses, as he is no longer, as a rule, called upon to think and create his work - a disastrous division of labour, with disastrous results,

Chapter X. Colours and Colouring

CLEAR and beautiful colouring, sometimes complex, sometimes simple, is one of the principal features of fine embroidery. Some people are by nature more of colourists than others, and often hit upon the right method of work, while they would be puzzled if you were to ask them to explain the why and wherefore of it ; but with others it is a matter of education, and a few general precepts founded on observation may be given for the benefit of those who are still feeling their way.

To the entirely uneducated eye (speaking with regard to colour) blue is blue, red is red, green, green, and so forth, every colour being positive, and there being no idea in the person's mind of the relation of one colour to another. But after a little observation and experiment you will find that beside their positive value, colours have a relative value of which you have never dreamed hitherto : a colour that is in itself beautiful may become absolutely atrocious by awkward handling, being placed, for example, beside some other shade that is its natural enemy.

Of the colours principally used for embroidery, blue is one of the pleasantest to have constantly under one's eye ; but personal idiosyncracies play an important part in colouring, and one person may declare against a generally admired colour without being able to explain the reason, though perhaps his doctor or his oculist could do so. Of blue choose those shades that have the pure, slightly grey, tone of indigo dye (varying somewhat, of course, on different materials). The quality of this colour is singularly beautiful, and not easy to describe except by negatives : it is neither slatey, nor too hot, nor too cold, nor does it lean to that unutterably coarse green-blue, libellously called ' peacock ' blue ; it has different tones - brilliant sometimes, and sometimes quiet - reminding one now of the grey-blue of a distant landscape, and now of the intense blue of a midday summer sky - if anything can resemble that.

Pure blues, such as I am attempting to describe, are to be seen in the Chinese silks and satins, which are familiar now to most of us, sometimes very pale, and sometimes almost black in their intensity, but always full and brilliant. The modifications of this blue to purple and grey-purple on the one side, and to green-blue on the other, are also useful colours, being chosen and employed with care.

Of reds, we have first a pure central red, between crimson and scarlet (for in the pure colour neither blue nor yellow should predominate), but this is a difficult shade to use; by far the most useful are those 'impure' shades which are modified by yellow, as, for instance, flesh-pink, salmon, orange, and scarlet; or by blue, as rose-pink, blood-red, and deep purple-red. The more delicate of such shades can be freely used where a central red, overpowering in its intensity, cannot. A warning, however, against abuse of warm orange and scarlet, which colours are the more valuable the more sparingly employed, and as dainty little spots of colour treasures indeed.

The most valuable colour next to blue is green, or, rather, equally valuable in its different way, being to some people more restful to the eye and brain. This being so, it is curious to remark how very rarely a good full green, neither muddy or coarse, is offered to the public. It is important for you to understand the different qualities of the various shades of green necessary for your work; for, if you are told, or if you feel that such and such is an intrinsically admirable colour, you may perhaps through sheer enthusiasm try to use it where it should not be used, or employ a certain shade in large masses that should be soberly dealt with, and so forth.

Here, again, we see the force of the positive and relative value of colours : a cold, strong green, not in itself very pleasing, placed against a clear brilliant yellow, gathers depth and force which it would otherwise lack ; a blue-green may strike the right note in a certain place, but if its use be exaggerated may blemish all. Now, there are certain greens which are brilliant and rich, and, when employed broken with other colours, produce a fine effect; but when a green is to be largely used, it should be chosen of a greyer, soberer shade, such as the eye rests on without fatigue. Avoid like poison the yellowish-brown green of a sickly hue that professes to be ' artistic,' and looks like nothing but corruption, and avoid also a hard metallic green, which, after all, would not easily seduce a novice, as it is very obtrusive in its unloveliness.

For your embroidery-palette certain definite sets of green will be necessary ; full, pure yellow-green, greyish-green, and blue-green, two or three shades of each. The brilliant pure green that we admire in a single spring leaf is impossible to use in large masses, nor does Nature, whose all-pervading colour is green, give us these acute notes in unbroken mass. You have only to look at the effect of light and shade in a tree in full spring foliage, with the browns and greys of its twigs, to realise this fact: the great masses of green meadow-land, besides showing a variety of colour that may be overlooked in a careless glance, have a tenderness of tone that is quite beyond and above any possible imitation in art.

For a central yellow choose a clear, full colour that is neither sickly and greenish, nor inclined to red and hot in tone. Of impure yellows, pale orange and a warm pinkish shade that inclines to copper are useful, besides the buff and brownish shades that will sometimes be wanted for special purposes. These, I think, include all the yellow shades that you need trouble about. A certain experience is wanted for the successful use of yellow, so that those who take a special delight in the intrinsic beauty of this fine colour will do well to avoid too enthusiastic an introduction of it into their work.

Of course, different colours and different dye-stuffs are affected by different materials. This is eminently the case with yellow: on wool, which absorbs the light, a large unbroken mass of yellow is positively forbidding; while in silk, with its lights and reflections that serve to break the colour, it is another matter.

Purple again is one of the 'difficult' colours with which we must, as it were, hit upon the exactly right tones to use. There are two valuable purples - a rather full red-purple, tending to russet, and a dusky grey-purple, which is, if the right tone is obtained, a very beautiful, and, if I may say so, poetic colour. Perhaps such colours belong more to the artist's palette than to the embroideress's set of wools or silks, but it seems to me there ought to be little difficulty in getting all manner of strange and charming shades out of the dyer's vat, if the dyer of commerce had the enthusiasm of his art.

Harmony, contrast, and repetition - all these laws that we have glanced at with regard to form have the same application to colouring. In arranging your work, you should have in your mind a definite scheme of colour, as simple as possible at first, and consisting, perhaps, merely of one predominating colour with a few touches of another for a relief. When a little more experienced, you should still have some dominating colour or shades of a colour, among which contrasting tones are placed, bringing out the relative values according to your skill or instinct in choosing.

For elaborate and costly work, it is obvious that gold and silver will form an important factor in the scheme of colour but here again it must be noted thatmetals, if employed in great masses, highly raised and without due relief and softening by colours, are apt to look hard and a trifle - sometimes more than a trifle - vulgar.

For example, compare a late French or Spanish vestment of the richest description with one of the same kind made in one of the best periods of this art. Both are equally lavish in materials and workmanship ; the modern is probably a mass of thick padded and corded gold, sewn down with yellow or white silk on a rich white ground. While labouring by this piling up of metal to get all the effect of splendour he possibly can out of his materials, the craftsman has produced a piece of work smart enough for theatrical effect, or for a piece of pageantry, but giving no idea of splendid and sumptuous beauty, such as the faithful of all times have been desirous of surrounding their religion with, according to their abilities. But, on the other hand, a similar work of art, wrought in a more spontaneous and genuine period, with similar aims, that is, to be a fit offering to a favourite saint, in whose benevolent personality the craftsman had a genuine belief, would have shown less vaunting of costly material - though none were stinted ; but the cunning with

Decorative Needlework

which rich and brilliant colours were interwoven with gold would leave an impression on the eye of subtlety and fantasy that is one of the charms of the art.

Some such work that I have in my mind has a flat, golden background, the surface broken by being worked in a simple zig-zag or waved pattern, needing far more 'technique' and delicacy than the lumpy gold of the late French or Spanish cited above. On this gold background will be placed subject groups from the lives of the Saints, perhaps, or rich and fanciful ornament and foliage, wrought finely and laboriously with silk, with more gold, and possibly with little pearls and other precious stones. You don't want to have your high priest look as if he were cut out of tin-foil, but clothed in changeful folds that shine as he moves, and take lights and shadows on them like those of precious stones themselves.

Such work, with its quality of mystery, had a living splendour, and was indeed 'fit for kings' treasuries,' as the simple saying has it, or as we might say nowadays, fit to gladden the eyes of all who believe that everything beautiful that is made serves its due purpose in enriching the treasury of the world.

I had no intention of raising the question here whether kings' treasuries or the treasury of humanity itself should have the privilege of possessing beautiful things, and. what is more, the power of enjoying them ; but a belief in the power of beauty is a wholesome thing, and I make no apology for preaching it by the way. As an art, therefore, that should help to decorate home life very largely, and public life too, as regards religious buildings, public halls on festive occasions, and so forth, embroidery deserves to be taken seriously, especially the higher branch of it, which includes intricate colour and work in gold and precious stones, such as that of which I have been speaking.

It is not easy to give much advice about method in colouring, as I suppose every one has his or her own pet way of setting to work. The colouring of your design can be treated as dark on a light ground, that is, using principally dark colours on a light ground ; or,

Decorative Needlework

as light upon dark, using light colours on a dark ground - a more effective and more difficult treatment ; or by placing colour upon colour, forming, as it were, a mosaic of colours of more or less equal tone. This last is an elaborate but very beautiful method, in which Eastern artists have always excelled. A few hints as to grouping of colours to guard against fundamental errors will be all that is possible to touch upon here.

As aforesaid, start with the simplest possible scheme of colour while you are feeling your way, and when you launch out into combinations of two or three colours, let one predominate, the others being rhythmically disposed to emphasise the leading tone. When you feel you can come to bolder contrasts, avoid placing a blue directly against a green of nearly the same tone ; if blue and green are mixed, the blue must be very light against a dark green, or the reverse. Again, red and yellow, if both vivid, will need a softening line to separate them, though a pale yellow with a clear, pure, rather delicate scarlet is by no means a displeasing arrangement ; or again, a full, clear yellow with a very pale brick-red.

Red and green must be carefully chosen, and softened by an outline ; avoid much use of any cold green, especially avoid placing it against a misty blue, for the indecision and muddled effect of this arrangement is the reverse of pleasant.

Brown must be carefully chosen, warm in tint, but not hot; a little of it will be necessary in figure-work, but for merely floral design a decided brown need be seldom used. Black also has distinct value in certain sorts of work, but the use of it should be left to an experienced hand.

In handling colours, you must bear in mind the retiring quality of some and the assertive quality of others, but do not emphasise these qualities too much. Your work should, on the whole, be very flat and quiet in general character, though as bright as you can get it in the individual tones. As in design, avoid confusion and indistinctness of detail. The mystery and reticence spoken of with regard to work of the highest order is quite another quality, and one with which we have little to do here, beyond teaching ourselves to recognise and appreciate it. Make no attempt to grope after 'startling novelties,' but try for pure, clear tones. When people say they like 'soft, quiet colouring' in textiles and embroidery, it is an unconscious tribute to harmonious colouring, for the colours themselves, if excellent in quality, can hardly be too brilliant ; if they appear so, it is the craftsman who is at fault.

In conclusion, I will ask leave to remind you that though there are the two aspects of embroidery, the one in which it is accepted as one of the lesser arts, having its due place in history and in our lives, and the other in which it serves as an occupation for an idle hour, yet in both cases it is worth nothing if not pursued with due method and soberness, and carried out in a workmanlike way.

Lightning Source UK Ltd.
Milton Keynes UK
UKOW051918250613

212810UK00001B/28/P